TWENTY TRUCKS PRESENTS

TRUCK TUNES™

45
TRUCK SONGS
TO SING ALOUD
TOGETHER

Jim Gardner and Rob Gardner
creators of the YouTube Channel TwentyTrucks

RP|KIDS
PHILADELPHIA

Running Press Kids
Hachette Book Group
1290 Avenue of the Americas, New York, NY 10104
www.runningpress.com/rpkids
@RP_Kids

Printed in China

First Edition: April 2023

Published by Running Press Kids, an imprint of Perseus Books, LLC, a subsidiary of Hachette Book Group, Inc. The Running Press Kids name and logo is a trademark of the Hachette Book Group.

The Hachette Speakers Bureau provides a wide range of authors for speaking events. To find out more, go to www.hachettespeakersbureau.com or call (866) 376-6591.

Additional Photography Credits:

Front cover images copyright © Getty Images: filonmar; fotostok_pdv

Back cover images copyright © Getty Images: Marco_Piunti; shaunl; byllwill

p. 13: Owned by BIGFOOT 4x4, Inc. Picture taken by Danny Maass; p. 27: Brundage-Bone Concrete Pumping; p. 33: AHMCT Research Center, University of California-Davis; p. 51: Image provided by Lindsay Transportation Solutions, LLC. Road Zipper is a trademark of Lindsay Transportation Solutions, LLC; p. 55: Sunbelt Drilling

Copyright © Getty Images: upsidedowndog p. 4; 2windspa p. 5; valio84sl p. 5; amriphoto p. 9; Marco_Piunti p. 11, 95; shaul p. 17, 95; Avalon_Studio p. 23, 95; Driendl Group p. 25, 95; Brian Stablyk p. 29; VisualCommunications p. 31; Photography taken by Mario Gutiérrez p. 35; fotog p. 41; wwing p. 43; byllwill p. 45; Huntstock p. 47; dlewis33 p. 53; Sergiy Trofimov Photography p. 59, 95; CUHRIG p. 71; Schroptschop p. 73; Captainflash p. 91; Chip Somodevilla / Staff p. 93; Tsezer, ArtStok, alano design throughout interior; Tsezer end sheets

Copyright © Shutterstock: Dmytro Budnik p. 7; Roman Zaiets p. 57, 95; TFoxFoto p. 61; Valentin Valkov p. 79, 95; Oleg Torino p. 81; F Armstrong Photography p. 87

Print book cover and interior design by Katie Benezra.

Library of Congress Control Number: 2022019524

ISBNs: 978-0-7624-8213-9 (hardcover), 978-0-7624-8214-6 (ebook)

APS

10 9 8 7 6 5 4 3 2 1

CONTENTS

INTRODUCTION

When my son, Pierce, was about two years old, he suddenly became very interested in trucks of all kinds, from pickups to dump trucks. As we drove around town, he would call out the names of the trucks he saw: "Hey, Daddy, there's a car carrier!" Soon his twin sister, Kassidy, joined in, and the two of them made it a competition to see who could locate and name trucks the fastest.

Growing up, I had my own unique experience with trucks and work machines. My grandfather owned a lumber yard, and my dad was a general contractor. When I was sixteen, I learned to drive a manual transmission on a small dump truck and worked on job sites driving a tractor.

As a parent, my kids' enthusiasm for trucks combined with my own experiences inspired me to create a video for young kids that would focus on real trucks at work. Because Pierce and Kassidy enjoyed counting and naming so much, I decided to name the video *Twenty Trucks*. As a key part of the production, I convinced my brother, Rob, who is a composer and talented musician, to write the theme song for *Twenty Trucks*.

Soon after releasing *Twenty Trucks*, we began receiving emails and handwritten letters from kids, parents, grandparents, and fans, asking for a sequel. Many of these fans provided their own suggestions for more trucks to include.

As we prepared to work on our next video, I had an idea that I pitched to my brother: What if we featured just ten new trucks but wrote a song for each one and called the video *Truck Tunes*? As part of my proposal, I assured Rob that I would write a first draft of the lyrics along with basic musical ideas for the chorus and verses. Rob agreed, and we began writing ten new songs.

Truck Tunes became a much bigger success than *Twenty Trucks* with our videos on YouTube and the truck songs on many streaming platforms. To date, we have released four more versions of *Truck Tunes* and have written more than sixty songs about all kinds of trucks and work machines.

For this book, we have selected forty-five of our favorite *Truck Tunes* songs. We hope that you will find many of your favorites here, too! Deciding which songs to select for the book was difficult, and we had to leave out many that mean a lot to us. There is a story behind each song and video. We are grateful for the many people—from vehicle operators to equipment manufacturers to family and friends—who helped us create these videos and songs.

Some of our *Truck Tunes* feature machines that may not technically be considered trucks. We have used the term *truck* very broadly and challenge you to determine which machines fit the definition. We hope that you will have fun reading (and singing) this book, while learning more about these amazing machines as they work and play.

—Jim Gardner

DUMP TRUCK

Dump, dump, dump, dump it
Dump it, Dump Truck
Dump, dump, dump, dump it
Dump it, Dump Truck
Dump, dump, dump, dump it
Dump it, Dump Truck
Oh, dump it

Loading up some boulders
Working with a loader
Or maybe even a backhoe, oh, oh
Grab an excavator
He'll do all the labor
And now we're ready
To load, load, load

So, load, load, load him up
Load the Dump Truck
Load, load, load him up
Load the Dump Truck
Load, load, load him up
Load the Dump Truck
Oh, load him up

So, what does he carry?
Well, anything that's heavy
Like these giant rocks, you know
Or lots of tiny pebbles
Thousands of tiny pebbles
And now we're ready
To back him up

So, back, back, back him up
Back the Dump Truck
Back, back, back him up
Back up Dump Truck
Back, back, back him up
Back the Dump Truck
Oh, back him up

Where does he get the strength
To lift his giant bed?
He must have a back of steel
He uses his hydraulic ram
To lift his bed, you see
With power extraordinary

So, dump, dump, dump, dump it
Dump it, Dump Truck
Dump, dump, dump, dump it
Oh, dump it, Dump Truck
Dump, dump, dump, dump it
Dump it, Dump Truck
Oh, dump it

You know, you know you got to dump
Dump, dump, dump, dump it
Dump it, Dump Truck
Dump, dump, dump, dump it

You know, you know you got to dump
Dump, dump, dump, dump it
Dump it, Dump Truck
Oh, dump it

EXCAVATOR

This is the work I really love
Because that's what an Excavator does
I said, this is the work I really love
Because that's what an Excavator does

He's an Excavator
His work is more like fun
He digs with his big bucket
And works out in the sun

He can dig the deepest
Holes that you have ever seen
Other trucks can dig, oh yes
But not like this machine
No, not like this machine

This is the work I really love
Because that's what an Excavator does
I said, this is the work I really love
Because that's what an Excavator does

See how long his boom is
Reaching far below
The tracks that keep him safe from
Falling in this deep, deep hole

One of his best talents
Is spinning all the way around
In either of both directions
His tracks stay firmly on the ground
Tracks stay firmly on the ground

This is the work I really love
Because that's what an Excavator does
I said, this is the work I really love
Because that's what an Excavator does

After a long day of
Hard and dusty, dusty work
He likes to take a shower
And spray off all that dirt

He'll start tomorrow early
Just as the new day dawns
And work a long, long day again
But you'll never see him yawn
You'll never see him yawn

This is the work I really love
Because that's what an Excavator does
I said, this is the work I really love
Because that's what an Excavator does
(Repeat)

FIRE TRUCK

Can you tell me where the fire is?
He will put it out
Call me on the radio
He will put it out
Need help with an emergency
He can help you out
Can you tell me where the fire is?
He will put it out

He gets the call
Loads up his crew
And sounds his horn
He's needed now
And this big truck
Has not a moment to lose

Flashes his lights
His sirens howl
Get out of his way
He's got to move
He's got to get there now

Can you tell me where the fire is?
He will put it out
Call me on the radio
He will put it out
Need help with an emergency
He can help you out

Can you tell me where the fire is?
He will put it out

Now at the fire
Unrolls his hose
And turns it on
The hydrant pumps
Some trucks add foam
To make the fire go out

With buildings tall
The flames stretch high
Get out of their way
The ladder climbs
Until it reaches the sky

To fight a blaze
He carries lots of gear
So the fire fighters
Can have no fear
He's well equipped
With pikes and poles
And axes so sharp
He's not afraid
This truck is in control

Can you tell me where the fire is?
He will put it out
Call me on the radio
He will put it out
Need help with an emergency

He can help you out
Can you tell me where the fire is?
He will put it out
(Repeat)

11

MONSTER TRUCK

There's a truck that's
Fast and loud
He's happiest when
He plays for a crowd

Doing wheelies and donuts
And jump after jump
He loves to do
All kinds of stunts

He's a brute
Some say a thug
Smashes little cars
Like they're little bugs

He might crash or flip
His tires might pop
Doesn't care much
He just won't stop

So, what would you call him?
When he's the toughest
When he's the baddest truck around
Call him a Monster, Monster Truck
Let them hear how you roar
Monster, Monster Truck
Meanest 4x4

He can jump
A giant plane
Yes, this truck is
Completely insane

In arenas and stadiums
What do they shout?
As they watch him
Drive about

What do they call him?
When he's the toughest
When he's the baddest truck around
They call him Monster, Monster Truck
Let them hear how you roar
Monster, Monster Truck
Meanest 4x4

And that's what they call him
'Cause he's the toughest
'Cause he's the baddest truck around
What they call him?
They call him Monster, Monster Truck
Let them hear how you roar
Monster, Monster Truck
Meanest 4x4

Monster, Monster Truck
Let them hear how you roar
Monster, Monster Truck
Meanest 4x4

POLICE VEHICLES

Just doing their job
On the streets day and night
Police trucks and cruisers
And fast motor bikes
Sounding their sirens
And flashing their lights
Just doing their job
Yeah, they're doing it right

What does he do on patrol?
Well, he's on the lookout for trouble, so
Listens close to the calls on his radio
And checks the data on his terminal

Oh, these cars aren't hard to identify
With their lights, their gear,
    and marks on every side
But when he is unmarked,
    well he just might hide
That is, until he turns on his lights

Just doing their job
On the streets day and night
Police trucks and cruisers
And fast motor bikes
Sounding their sirens
And flashing their lights
Just doing their job
Yeah, they're doing it right

Look! Here's a police SUV
Oh, her size gives her more functionality
She can load up more gear,
    leaving nothing behind
Has plenty of room for this special K9

When she's asked to take a call off-road
Oh, she's got all the clearance to go,
    you know
Oh she's brave, and she's strong
    and professional
There aren't many places she can't
    easily go

Just doing their job
On the streets day and night
Police trucks and cruisers
And fast motor bikes
Sounding their sirens
And flashing their lights
Just doing their job
Yeah, they're doing it right

Here's one more vehicle
It's the fast and agile police motorcycle
Who is quick to respond to an
    accident scene
They're skilled and alert,
    prepared for anything

To stay cool means lots of practice,
    you know
It takes training for every scenario
So they all have their own
    special facilities
Where they work to improve
    their abilities

Just doing their job
On the streets day and night
Police trucks and cruisers
And fast motor bikes
Sounding their sirens
And flashing their lights
Just doing their job
Yeah, they're doing it right
(Repeat)

CEMENT MIXER

Starting the day
Under the hopper
Loading up with
Sand, gravel, cement, and water

Hitting the road
Driving round while he mixes
Needs to make sure
That the concrete stays viscous

Cement Mixer
Round and round, he turns his big drum
Cement Mixer
Round and round, pours concrete by the ton
Cement Mixer
Round and round, works till the job's done
He goes round and round and round
And round and round

Backing up now
In just the right direction
Adding the chutes
To get the proper extension

Pouring fast now
Controls the flow with his levers
Swinging from one side
And back to the other

Cement Mixer
Round and round, he turns his big drum
Cement Mixer
Round and round, pours concrete by the ton
Cement Mixer
Round and round, works till the job's done
He goes round and round and round
And round and round and round and round
And round and round

Cleaning up now
Spraying off all the cement
Loading the chutes
In their proper placement

Driving back to
The plant for more concrete
Doing just what
It takes to get the job complete

Cement Mixer
Round and round, he turns his big drum
Cement Mixer
Round and round, pours concrete by the ton
Cement Mixer
Round and round, works till the job's done
He goes round and round and round
And round and

Cement Mixer
Round and round, he turns his big drum
Cement Mixer
Round and round, pours concrete by the ton
Cement Mixer
Round and round, works till the job's done

He goes round and round and round
And round and round and round and round
And round and round and round and round
And round and round

GARBAGE TRUCK

Garbage, refuse, trash, or waste
For all these things, he has a taste
Bet there's a Garbage Truck
That works near you
At the job he loves to do

Look! If you watch
Then you'll see him weekly
If he could talk
Well, then he'd say, "Feed me"
All of the stuff
That you just don't need, he
Gobbles it up
Like a sweet, sweet treat
Gobbles it up
Like a sweet, sweet treat

Garbage, refuse, trash, or waste
For all these things, he has a taste
Bet there's a Garbage Truck
That works near you
At the job he loves to do

He lifts containers
Or cans that's easy
With grapple arms
Or forks like these, he
Puts everything in

A hopper in back
Then smashes it up
To make it compact
Smashes it up
To make it compact

Garbage, refuse, trash, or waste
For all these things, he has a taste
Bet there's a Garbage Truck
That works near you
At the job he loves to do

At the end of the day
When he's all filled up, he
Heads to the landfill
Some call it the dump
When he backs up, beeping
Pushing trash in a block
Then he's back on the road
Making all his stops
He's back on the road
Making all his stops
He's back on the road
Making all his stops

Garbage, refuse, trash, or waste
For all these things, he has a taste
Bet there's a Garbage Truck
That works near you
At the job he loves to do
(Repeat)

TOW TRUCK

When a car is down on its luck
When it breaks, overheats, or gets stuck
That's when she does her stuff
And her stuff is more than enough
That's when you call, when you call,
   when you call a Tow Truck

When we're talking Tow Trucks
Well, there are different types
This one's a flatbed
That's because her bed is flat
Her bed can roll back, can roll back
   or slide, oh!

Then the car she's giving a tow
Is all prepared to go
You gotta know, gotta know
How she's gonna go go
It's pulled up with a winch
It makes her job a cinch
That's why you call, why you call,
   why you call out for a tow

T-tow, T-tow, T-tow, T-tow, T-tow,
   T-tow, T-tow, T-tow, T-tow, T-tow
Tow Truck
T-tow, T-tow, T-tow, T-tow, T-tow
Tow Truck

Now this truck is no joke
See her lift with a boom and a yoke
We call her a wheel-lift
That's because she lifts the wheels
Her hoist is powerful, powerful,
   she's got power, oh!

Which side is she liftin'?
Well, you know, it all depends
She's good to go, good to go no
   matter what you need to tow
Rear drive, she lifts the back
Front drive, the front's where it's at
She makes the call, makes the call,
   makes the call, for the tow

T-tow, T-tow, T-tow, T-tow, T-tow,
   T-tow, T-tow, T-tow, T-tow, T-tow
Tow Truck
T-tow, T-tow, T-tow, T-tow, T-tow
Tow Truck

Drive me safely home, Tow Truck
Drive me safely home
Drive me safely home, Tow Truck
Drive me safely home

When a car is down on its luck
When it breaks, overheats, or gets stuck

That's when she does her stuff
And her stuff is more than enough
That's when you call, when you call,
   when you call a Tow Truck

T-tow, T-tow, T-tow, T-tow, T-tow,
   T-tow, T-tow, T-tow, T-tow, T-tow
Tow Truck

T-tow, T-tow, T-tow, T-tow, T-tow
Tow Truck

Drive me safely home, Tow Truck
Drive me safely home
Drive me safely home, Tow Truck
Drive me safely home

21

BULLDOZER

They call him Bulldozer
Or just Dozer for short
And every morning
For work he'll report
To shove big loads of
Dirt and rocks all around
And drag his ripper
To tear up the ground

Like an enormous, crazy caterpillar
He is the meanest
Toughest of all tractors
Known as a crawler
He's so good at his work
Uses his ripper
To break the hardest earth

They call him Bulldozer
Or just Dozer for short
And every morning
For work he'll report
To shove big loads of
Dirt and rocks all around
And drag his ripper
To tear up the ground

To do his moving, he uses a blade
It's made of metal
Some call it a plate

In back the ripper
Can have one or more shanks
These trucks are so tough
They could tow a tank

They call him Bulldozer
Or just Dozer for short
And every morning
For work he'll report
To shove big loads of
Dirt and rocks all around
And drag his ripper
To tear up the ground

Their tracks of steel can work any terrain
They are so strong that
It boggles the brain
Working with Scrapers
And with Graders too
They clear the land, and
Oh they do it so soon

They call him Bulldozer
Or just Dozer for short
And every morning
For work he'll report
To shove big loads of
Dirt and rocks all around
And drag his ripper
To tear up the ground

They can push or pull other big rigs
And help them out
So they can dig and dig
The most stubborn dirt
And stone that's known
Or if they need to
They can work all alone

They call him Bulldozer
Or just Dozer for short
And every morning
For work he'll report
To shove big loads of
Dirt and rocks all around
And drag his ripper
To tear up the ground
(Repeat)

TRACTOR TRAILER

Well, he's got so many, many names
With all that he gets done
There ain't no way he'd ever be as
Happy with just one

Some call him a Tractor Trailer
And that's certainly true
Then there's Big Rig, Semi Truck
And 18-Wheeler too

So, why do they call him a
    Tractor Trailer?
He's got a Tractor out in front
That's where the driver sits
It pulls the Trailer in the back
'Cause that's where his cargo fits
And that's why they call him a
    Tractor Trailer

Yeehaw! Tractor Trailer

Now, what about Big Rig?
Well, the Tractor part is made to pull
And some call that a Rig
You need a ladder to get in
Because this truck is so darn big
And that's why they call it a Big Rig

Oh, he's got so many, many names
With all that he gets done
Well, there ain't no way he'd ever be as
Happy with just one

We know he's a Tractor Trailer
And that's certainly true
But this Big Rig is a Semi Truck
And an 18-Wheeler too

So, how about Semi Truck?
The Trailer has no wheels in front
'Cause that's where he hooks up
Well, semi means a half a thing
So he's a Semi Truck
'Cause he pulls with him half a truck

Oh yeah! Wooeee! He's pulling
    two trailers
That's a double

Can you guess why they call him an
    18-Wheeler?
Well, that's how many wheels he's got
With nine wheels on each side
Some trucks have less
And some have more
And some are extra wide
This big truck has twenty-five

Wait! That's twenty-six
My mistake

Oh, he's got so many, many names
With all the work he does
There ain't no way he'd ever be as
Happy with just one

No, he wouldn't be happy
With just one

CONCRETE BOOM PUMP

Working early in the morning
Starting out at day's first light
He's got a lot of work to do, yeah
And he works with all of his might

Once at the work site, he sets things up
Carefully getting his outriggers placed
He'll be pumping tons of concrete,
    pumping tons of concrete all day
So he's gotta have a steady base

Concrete Pump
Concrete Pump Boo-oo-oom
Concrete Boom Pump
Concrete Pump, Concrete Pump
Boo-oo-oom, Boo-oo-oom

Mix trucks load up the concrete
His hopper's filled again and again
Then from this central location
He reaches out his boom and extends

He manages the pour from below
Properly regulating how it flows
He maneuvers his robotic, maneuvers
    his robotic arm, oh

Yeah, it's guided by remote control

Concrete Pump
Concrete Pump Boo-oo-oom
Concrete Boom Pump
Concrete Pump, Concrete Pump
Boo-oo-oom, Boo-oo-oom

Some trucks boast impressive
    pump rates
Beyond a hundred yards for every hour
The pressure this requires is great
It takes a massive surplus of power

See how his arms have multiple parts
Each one articulated and so strong
Flexible joints keep them together, his
    joints keep them together, and woh!
Some arms are two hundred feet long!

Concrete Pump, Concrete Pump
Boo-oo-oom
Concrete Boom Pump
Concrete Pump, Concrete Pump
Boo-oo-oom, Boo-oo-oom
(Repeat)

AMBULANCE

The Ambulance is racing
She's speeding to the scene
Her sirens blare, her lights go flash
And this is what they mean:

Watch out! An Ambulance is coming
Watch out! An Ambulance is coming

When someone is in trouble
They dial 9-1-1
She gets the call, and moves along
'Cause now she's on the run

She's loaded up with equipment
To help somebody out
She's got the stuff to fix you up
She knows the fastest route!

Move, move outta her way
So she can get there fast
It's an emergency
And she has gotta get past

Watch out! An Ambulance is coming
Watch out! An Ambulance is coming

The person she is helping
Is loaded up in back
The doors get closed and off they go
To the hospital, just like that

If someone's in a position
With an urgent condition
Where there's not a physician
She can do great things

Yeah, she is not a magician
No, but helping people's her mission
She has got an
Emergency Medical Technician

Move, move outta her way
So she can get there fast
It's an emergency
And she has gotta get past
(Repeat)

Watch out! An Ambulance is coming
Watch out! An Ambulance is coming
Watch out! An Ambulance is coming
Watch out! An Ambulance is coming

SNOW PLOW

Snow Plow
Snow Plow

When it comes to snow removal
Snow Plow
Sure to meet with your approval
Snow Plow

He lowers his blade down to the ground
To shovel away the snow that's falling
Down, down, down
Snow Plow

To give drivers better traction
Snow Plow
He knows just the proper action
Snow Plow

Sand and cinder he lays down
    on the ground
Making driving more safe when
    snow is falling
Down, down, down
Snow Plow

But, Snow Plow, how now can you see
With all that snow and storm debris?
He uses good technology
To show him where the lanes should be

If the snow falls really heavy
Snow Plow
Might see his buddies getting ready
Snow Plow

Dozers and Loaders and Graders
    come round
And Excavators while snow is falling
Down, down, down
Snow Plow

But, Snow Plow, how now can you go
With mounds of snow piled high and low?
His friend Snow Blower blows the snow
And helps the Snow Plow clear the road

A blizzard got you in a pickle?
Snow Plow
You need this Winter Storm Vehicle
Snow Plow

Just what would we do when storms
    come 'round
If we didn't have you when snow is falling
Down, down, down
Snow Plow

When snow is falling
Down, down, down
Snow Plow

When snow is falling
Down, down, down

31

VACUUM TRUCK

Just like the machine
That you use in your home
His job is to clean
He's much bigger, though

Yeah, he can suck up this junk
With his high-suction hose
It looks like a trunk
Yeah, like an elephant nose
Just like an elephant nose

So, swing, swing your hose
Like an elephant trunk
Clean up the road
Suck up all of the junk

Swing back and forth
And with any luck
You'll clean up
Like a Vacuum Truck

He drives down the road
Finding trash to clean up
He moves oh so slowly
He's not in a rush

He works by controls
That look almost the same
As the kind you use
Playing a video game
Just like a video game

So, swing, swing your hose
Like an elephant trunk
Clean up the road
Suck up all of the junk

Swing back and forth
And with any luck
You'll clean up
Like a Vacuum Truck

Let's hear you do it
Make the sound that he makes
A whoosh or a shoosh
Is all that it takes

And we'll watch him as he works
He'll leave us all awed
He's got enough power
To suck up a dirt clod
Yeah, a big dirt clod
Wow, that's a huge dirt clod!

Well, that's just impressive

So, swing, swing your hose
Like an elephant trunk
Clean up the road
Suck up all of the junk

Swing back and forth
And with any luck
You'll clean up
Like a Vacuum Truck

Let's see you swing it
Like an elephant trunk
Let's see you clean up
Suck up all of the junk

Swing it back and forth
And with any luck
You'll clean up
Like a Vacuum Truck
You'll clean up
Like a Vacuum Truck

BUS

Don't have a car?
No need to fuss
Can't drive a truck?
Just take a Bus

No train nearby?
Come ride with us
Don't want to fly?
Hop on a Bus

Let's say you got to get to school
Wouldn't riding with your friends be cool?
A School Bus picks you up first thing
Gets you to class before the school
    bell rings

When the Bus picks you up or
    drops you off
She goes and puts out a sign,
    so traffic stops
Her flashing lights alert drivers
    to watch out!
Because the kids' safety is paramount
I say the kids' safety is paramount

Don't have a car?
No need to fuss
Can't drive a truck?
Just take a Bus

No train nearby?
Come ride with us
Don't want to fly?
Hop on a Bus

A City Bus can take you anywhere
You step right in, and you pay your fare
And you could take your bike along
Right in front of the Bus is where
    it belongs

These Buses are so strong, they're so
    very strong
See how this Bus is two cars—one, two—
    two cars long?
Some are powered by fuels like gas,
    and see
How this Bus gets its strength
    from electricity
It gets its strength from electricity

Don't have a car?
No need to fuss
Can't drive a truck?
Just take a Bus

No train nearby?
Come ride with us
Don't want to fly?
Hop on a Bus

Well, a Passenger Bus makes longer trips
Down highways and freeways you can
    see them zip
They take you far away to other towns
The perfect truck to get you around

And lookee here, lookee here,
    this one's designed
With all the sight-seeing tourists
    well in mind
Some have two levels where you can sit
They call these double-deckers
They call them double-deckers

They call them double-deckers and
    they're legit

Don't have a car?
No need to fuss
Can't drive a truck?
Just take a Bus

No train nearby?
Come ride with us
Don't want to fly?
Hop on a Bus
(Repeat)

35

SKIDSTEER

How does this truck steer
When his wheels only go straight?
He's able to turn thanks to a trick
That's his namesake

When his right wheels go faster than
    his left
The left skids and he turns left
When his left side wins, he turns right
Just like you might have guessed
Just watch him pirouette!

He loves to show off what he can do
Doing tricks while he gets work done
Doesn't stop till the job is through
No, the Skidsteer is just the one
Who's always having fun
Skidsteer is always having fun
Skidsteer is always having fun

There aren't many jobs
He won't easily tackle
Like tearing down a wall
With the help of a grapple

Even though he may seem pretty small
Skidsteer's one tough cat
This one here has solid tires
That never will go flat

He loves to show off what he can do
Doing tricks while he gets work done
Doesn't stop till the job is through
No, the Skidsteer is just the one
Who's always having fun
Skidsteer is always having fun
Skidsteer is always having . . .

He's so functional
That the others can't compete
See him using forks to break up
Asphalt and concrete

His attachments make him versatile
But there's one that he likes best
That's right, it's his bucket
He just thinks it's handiest

He loves to show off what he can do
Doing tricks while he gets work done
Doesn't stop till the job is through
No, the Skidsteer is just the one
Who's always having fun
Skidsteer is always having fun
Skidsteer is always having fun
Skidsteer is always having fun
Skidsteer is always having fun

BUCKET TRUCK

Lifting up, up, up in a B-b-bucket Truck
Climbing high, high, high in the sky-y
When it's tough, tough, tough
And a ladder's not enough
You need a b-b-b-b-bucket
A bucket on a truck

Need to trim your trees?
He makes it such a breeze
Fixing lights and wires
He climbs high, high, higher

Hanging cable too?
Well, he is able to
Strong like a table, too
And just as stable too

But so that you don't fall
A harness is a good call
When on a Bucket Truck
Aerial Bucket Truck
Oh, he's a Bucket Truck
Climb in a Bucket Truck

Lifting up, up, up in a B-b-bucket Truck
Climbing high, high, high in the sky-y
When it's tough, tough, tough
And a ladder's not enough

You need a b-b-b-b-bucket
A bucket on a truck

He's got some other names
Some call them Bucket Cranes
Or why not Cherry Picker?
Lifting workers quicker

Need to be elevated?
Your lift accelerated?
He's got it regulated
Don't underestimate it

His hydraulics go
Controlled above and below
'Cause he's a Bucket Truck
Aerial Bucket Truck
Yeah, he's a Bucket Truck
Or some say Basket Truck

And it's important to be smart
Thinking safety from the start
Oh, especially when working with wires
Beware the w-w-wires!

So, you put on rubber gloves
While you work high up above
Yeah, 'cause that's what
    electricity requires!
Be careful up there!

When lifting up, up, up in a
    B-b-bucket Truck
Climbing high, high, high in the sky-y
When it's tough, tough, tough
And a ladder's not enough
You need a b-b-b-b-bucket
A bucket on a truck
A bucket on a truck

Oh, lifting up, up, up in a
    B-b-bucket Truck
Climbing high, high, high in the sky-y
When it's tough, tough, tough
And a ladder's not enough
You need a b-b-b-b-bucket
A bucket on a truck
A bucket on a truck

CAR CARRIER

May take all day
Might drive all night
Gotta get those cars
To their destination alright

Gotta drive with care
Can't drive too fast
And secure each one
With chains and ratchets and with straps

If you need to move your car
And you just don't want to drive
There's a truck you want to call

If driving cross the country
Seems a great big barrier
The answer's easy
Use a Car Carrier

If the car's your baby
And there's nothing scarier
Than letting go
Go on and he'll take care of her
No need to worry
He's a Car Carrier

The upper deck
Is lowered now

Every car is placed
And then it's tied securely right down

The level on top
Now slowly lifts
Hydraulically
So the others all can fit

If you need to move your car
And you just don't want to drive
There's a truck you want to call

If driving cross the country
Seems a great big barrier
The answer's easy
Use a Car Carrier

If the car's your baby
And there's nothing scarier
Than letting go
Go on and he'll take care of her
No need to worry
He's a Car Carrier

Just how many
Cars can it hold?
Can you count them
All the cars new and old

Could it be nine?
No, count again

It's smart design
Means it actually fits ten

*'Cause if driving cross the country
Seems a great big barrier
The answer's easy
Use a Car Carrier*

*If the car's your baby
And there's nothing scarier
Than letting go
Go on and he'll take care of her
No need to worry
He's a Car Carrier*

It may look crowded
But the more the merrier
Just keep on loading
He's a Car Carrier

*If the car's your baby
And there's nothing scarier
Than letting go
Go on and he'll take care of her
No need to worry
He's a Car Carrier
No need to worry
He's a Car Carrier*

AIRCRAFT DEICER

B-R-R-R, B-R-R-R, Deicer
It's so cold!
At 32 degrees and below
Water freezes, you know
Turns into ice and to snow
B-R-R-R, B-R-R-R, Deicer!

The weather for flying could be nicer
But thanks to the Aircraft Deicer
Planes can take off safely and ice-free
No matter how freezing cold it might be
So fly on airplane, fly with me!

Oh-oh-oh!

B-R-R-R, B-R-R-R, Deicer
It's so cold!
At 32 degrees and below
Water freezes, you know
Turns into ice and to snow
B-R-R-R, B-R-R-R, Deicer!

Before spraying the planes all down
She fills up with a special compound
Water and glycol when mixed together
Just won't freeze in the coldest
     of weather

She does her job in two stages, you see
First, she removes all the ice thoroughly
Then anti-icing is applied to prevent
Any ice from forming on the plane
     once again

B-R-R-R, B-R-R-R, Deicer
It's so cold!
At 32 degrees and below
Water freezes, you know
Turns into ice and to snow
B-R-R-R, B-R-R-R, Deicer!
(Repeat)

PICKUP TRUCK

They come in all sizes
Shapes, colors, and styles
They're rugged,
    they're tough
They can rack up
    the miles

These are hard-working
    trucks
Never down on their luck

Their tires are big, small
Or somewhere between
Got so many skills can
Do most anything

Just name something
    they can't do
Oh go on, I dare you!

Grandpa calls his a
Pick 'em up truck
Takes it off road
Don't ever get stuck

Says it's the ride he
Can always trust
Try to keep up, you'll be
Eatin' his dust

He's a Pickup,
    a Pickup Truck

And for some
    working trucks
A bed is just not enough
So some sport a rack to
Hold ladders and stuff

And when his rack's
    loaded down
No trouble getting
    around

To be fully equipped add
A toolbox to the mix
And make sure
    that there's
Not a thing you can't fix

Load up all your
    gear inside
Go on, give it a try

Grandpa calls his a
Pick 'em up truck
Takes it off road
Don't ever get stuck

Says it's the ride he
Can always trust
Try to keep up, you'll be
Eatin' his dust

He's a Pickup,
    a Pickup Truck
A Pickup, a Pickup Truck

Don't get me wrong
It's not all about work
These trucks have
    fun, too
They're perfect
    for camping
Or a trip to the dunes

Can tow a boat trailer
Or pull an RV
For extra towing power
You might want a dually
'Cause that's a Pickup
    with 4 wheels in back
Yippee, yippee!

Grandpa calls his a
Pick 'em up truck
Takes it off road
Don't ever get stuck

Says it's the ride he
Can always trust
Try to keep up, you'll be
Eatin' his dust

He's a Pickup, a Pickup . . .

A Pick 'em up truck
Takes it off road
Don't ever get stuck

Says it's the ride he
Can always trust

Try to keep up, you'll be
Eatin' his dust

He's a Pickup,
   a Pickup Truck

FRONT END LOADER

Loaders often work with Dump Trucks
Helping them to fill their beds up
With rocks and gravel and other stuff

Others might be better at digging holes
But no one loads a load like a
    Loader loads
And they can play many other roles

Because there isn't any on the road
As good at loading heavy loads
Front End Loader, you're as good as gold

This truck is cleaning up the
    messy debris
Of bark and wood from all the
    fallen trees
Pushing and scooping it up with ease

Watch now as this real big loader feeds
A bucket full of little rocks that will be
Crushed to sand in this machine

Oh no, there isn't any on the road
As good at scooping up a load
Front End Loader, you're as good as gold

Here's another trick this loader can do
He can work just like a Forklift, too
With this tool he can remove

And then with a very simple move
He can reattach his bucket to
His arms we call the boom

Working far away in a wooded grove
A loader uses grapple hooks to hold
These logs that finish up the load

Oh no, there isn't any on the road
As good at finding ways to load
Front End Loader, you're as good as gold

Oh no, there isn't any on the road
As good at loading heavy loads
As good at scooping up a load
As good at finding ways to load
There isn't any on the road
As good at helping trucks to load
Front End Loader, you're as good as gold

TRUCK CRANE

He's a Truck Crane
Lifting up his cargo
Truck Crane
Reach into the sky
Truck Crane
No one else can go so high,
    high, high, high

He shows up at the job site
Finds a spot that's just right
And way before noon, oh
He's working his telescoping boom

Outriggers are out
They'll keep him locked down
And hold him steady, oh
And now he's ready, oh
Tell me who's ready

He's a Truck Crane
Lifting up his cargo
Truck Crane
Reach into the sky
Truck Crane
No one else can go so high,
    high, high, high

His cable's in position
Lifting with precision
The hook block's now secure
He's good at this, for sure

The winch will wind up
Carefully he lines up
The boom extends far out
Sets the load on the ground
He sets it on the ground

He's a Truck Crane
Lifting up his cargo
Truck Crane
Reach into the sky
Truck Crane
No one else can go so high,
    high, high, high
(Repeat)

Strong like you can't believe
Tons of capacity
Whatever the job needs
Look how he lifts this tree

When the job is complete
A full day in the heat
He loads up everything
And heads home to his fleet

He's a Truck Crane
Lifting up his cargo
Truck Crane
Reach into the sky

Truck Crane
No one else can go so high,
high, high, high
(Repeat)

ROAD ZIPPER

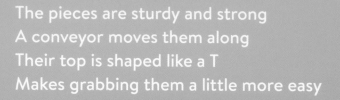

The Zip-Zip-Zip-Zip-Zipper Truck
Protecting two-way traffic
Zip-zip-zip-zip-zipping up
The wall from side-to-side
He's lift-lift-lift-lift-lifting up
With strength that's so fantastic
Switch-switch-switch-switch-switching up
The direction people drive

The Barrier Transfer Machine
Moves heavy lengths of concrete
Pins them together, creates
A barrier wall, curved or straight

Working hard in construction zones
Helping the traffic to flow
Rearranging lanes rapidly
In bridges, tunnels

You're the Road Zipper
A heavy lifter
You're a lane shifter
Such a sight to see
Oh, you're a rearranger
A game changer
You're a life saver
Most definitely

The pieces are sturdy and strong
A conveyor moves them along
Their top is shaped like a T
Makes grabbing them a little more easy

One pass can move 30 feet
Placed down without hurting the street
They work so efficiently
Wave hello and say

You're the Road Zipper
A heavy lifter
You're a lane shifter
Such a sight to see
Oh, you're a rearranger
A game changer
You're a life saver
Most definitely

The Zip-Zip-Zip-Zip-Zipper Truck
Protecting two-way traffic
Zip-zip-zip-zip-zipping up
The wall from side-to-side
He's lift-lift-lift-lift-lifting up
With strength that's so fantastic
Switch-switch-switch-switch-switching up
The direction people drive

Pick it up
Put it down
Keeping drivers safe and sound

Move it left
Move it right
Keeping traffic nice and tight
(Repeat)

The Zip-Zip-Zip-Zip-Zipper Truck
Protecting two-way traffic
Zip-zip-zip-zip-zipping up
The wall from side-to-side
He's lift-lift-lift-lift-lifting up
With strength that's so fantastic

Switch-switch-switch-switch-switching up
The direction people drive

You're the Road Zipper
A heavy lifter
You're a lane shifter
Such a sight to see
Oh, you're a rearranger
A game changer
You're a life saver
Most definitely
(Repeat)

51

STREET SWEEPER

He sweeps the street
Cleans up debris
He helps us keep
Our roads and
Parking lots so clean
He sweeps the street

He sweeps the street
So nice and neat
His bristly brooms
Sweep while he moves
They spin and spin
And spin again

'Cause that's the way he sweeps
    the street
Yes, that's the way he sweeps the street

He sweeps the street
Cleans up debris
He helps us keep
Our roads and
Parking lots so clean
He sweeps the street

He sprays the road
Each little hose
Shoots water 'round
And wets the ground

It keeps the dust
From flying up

And that's the way he sprays the road
Yes, that's the way he sprays the road

He sweeps the street
Cleans up debris
He helps us keep
Our roads and
Parking lots so clean
He sweeps the street

He dumps his bin
And lifts it then
It's called a hopper
Yes, that's his hopper
Pours out a hunk
Of dirt and junk

Oh, that's the way he dumps his bin
Yes, that's the way he dumps his bin

So every day
In his own way
He's out there sweeping
Simply keeping
Roads so clean
For you and me

'Cause that's the way he does this thing
Yes, that's the way he does this thing

He sweeps the street
Cleans up debris

He helps us keep
Our roads and
Parking lots so clean
He sweeps the street
(Repeat)

MOBILE DRILLING RIG

Drill it! Rig it!
Drill it! Rig it!
Then move it around
(Repeat)

Water in the desert
Can be difficult to find
He has to work so very hard
His bit will spin and hammer in time

And if the source is
A thousand feet below the well
He may load up fifty
Drill rods in his drilling carousel

Yes, he's a Mobile Drilling Rig
Guess how deep down he can dig?
He bores deep into the ground
Several hundred meters down

If you can dig it
Then he can dig it
If you can dig it
Then move it around

The main parts of the derrick
Are the boom and the mast
They supply the drilling skills
That cannot be copied or surpassed

The mast with its pulleys
Is the tallest part of the rig
And this truck has a boom
That sports a swinging, swinging jib

Oh, he's a Mobile Drilling Rig
Guess how deep down he can dig?
He bores deep into the ground
Several hundred meters down

If you can dig it
Then he can dig it
If you can dig it
Then move it around

Air and water remove
The cuttings the drill creates
And they help to cool the heat
That all the boring generates

He gets assistance
From some helpful machines
A compressor gives compressed air
And a pump gives all the water he needs

Some rigs have wheels
And they can transport themselves
Other rigs are tracked
And so they need a healthy big rig
    to help

Though the tracked rigs may not
Drive on the open road
At work they're very nimble
As these moves will clearly show

Oh, *he's a Mobile Drilling Rig*
Guess how deep down he can dig?

He bores deep into the ground
Several hundred meters down

If you can dig it
Then he can dig it
If you can dig it
Then move it around
(Repeat)

FORKLIFT

Let's do the Forklift Boogie
Lift it up, set it down
Back it up, turn around
The Forklift Boogie, yeah!

Oh, let's all do the Forklift Boogie
Back and forth and up and down
For a job like pallet moving
A better truck cannot be found

See how high he lifts this crate up
Then so gently pulls his blades
He doesn't want anything to break up
That's just how a Forklift's made

So do the Forklift Boogie
Lift it up, set it down
Back it up, turn around
The Forklift Boogie, yeah!

A pallet's made so his forks can
    fit through
Without any difficulty
Watch as this truck driver gets to
Line them up almost perfectly

Forklifts work in warehouses
At construction sites and lumberyards
There you'll see large stacks of pallets
You won't have to look too hard

To do the Forklift Boogie
Lift it up, set it down
Back it up, turn around
The Forklift Boogie, yeah!

He can lift such heavy loads that
He has to have a counterweight in back
This is so he won't tip over
Sometimes it's a battery pack

And in case things come a-tumblin' down
The forklift has an overhead guard
It protects the driver as he
Delivers his load In the lumberyard

So do the Forklift Boogie
Lift it up, set it down
Back it up, turn around

Again!

Lift it up, set it down
Back it up, turn around
The Forklift Boogie, yeah!

The Forklift Boogie, everyone!
Come back and do it with me again
sometime real soon now

ROAD ROLLER

Rollin' slowly, rollin' slowly
Rollin' slowly just to firm up the ground
She is rollin' slowly, rollin' slowly
Rollin' slowly just to firm up the ground

Just watch as she compacts
Hardens all the surface on initial contact
Her main job is to make the ground
   much more dense
The soil and asphalt become
   really intense

She'll have one or maybe two big drums
When there's one call it a single and with
   two a tandem
And these drums can each weigh a ton
   or two
Yeah, 'cause they have some tough and
   major rolling to do

Oh, she's rollin' slowly, rollin' slowly
Rollin' slowly just to firm up the ground
She is rollin' slowly, rollin' slowly
Rollin' slowly just to firm up the ground

She's careful and sure
Her work will endure
'Cause she's rollin' slowly just to firm up
   the ground

She is heavy and mean
A road rollin' machine
Oh, she's rollin' slowly just to firm up
   the ground

Someone much older than you
Might just call this truck a Steam
   Roller, too
Because they used to run on steam,
   as a rule
But today they run mainly on diesel fuel

Now, some drums are static and
   some vibrate
All that shake-shake-shakin' gives her
   more weight
There are some who add water for the
   same effect
When it comes to rolling rolling, she has
   our respect

'Cause she's rollin' slowly, rollin' slowly
Rollin' slowly just to firm up the ground
She is rollin' slowly, rollin' slowly
Rollin' slowly just to firm up the ground

She's careful and sure
Her work will endure
'Cause she's rollin' slowly just to firm up
   the ground

She is heavy and mean
A road rollin' machine
Oh, she's rollin' slowly just to firm up
   the ground

She is slow and she's cool
She's handy and you'll

Soon be rollin' slowly just to firm up
   the ground

She is heavy and mean
A road rollin' machine
Oh, she's rollin' slowly just to firm up
   the ground

PAVER

Making smooth roads
Well, that is his thing
He's a Paver you know
A hot paving machine

The dump truck, he provides
The material, material supply
Of the asphalt that he loads up high
Into the hopper on one side

And the conveyor moves all the while
So the auger can stockpile
The asphalt for the screed
That spreads with smoothest style

Making smooth roads
Oh, well that is his thing
And wherever you go
While out driving, you sing
He's a Paver you know
A hot paving machine

He's got no need, no need for speed
'Cause he's constant, and he's
    steady indeed
He may look slow, but that's how he goes
To be certain to maintain control

With weight and intense heat
He lays down a smooth street
He might use a tamper bar
To get the job complete

Making smooth roads
Oh, well that is his thing
And wherever you go
While out driving, you sing
He's a Paver you know
A hot paving machine

Well, he's real smart, make no mistake
To work all the calculations he makes
Figures the slope out, and he works out
    the crown
And the super, superelevation

Oh, the Paver works so well
That when roller comes to help
You might just hear him say
"I can do this by myself!"

Making smooth roads
Oh, well that is his thing
And wherever you go
While out driving, you sing
He's a Paver you know
A hot paving machine

SNOWCAT

Check out this
Amazing snow machine
Who without his tracks
He couldn't do a thing
Woh -oh
Not in the snow

They keep his footprint light
His ground pressure low
So he doesn't get stuck
In the deepest snow
No, no
Not in the snow

Hey, Hey, Hey!

With his special skills
He goes grooming all the hills
He's a Snowcat, oh!
Working through the night
Sculpting, shaping powder right
He's a Snowcat, oh, oh, oh, oh, oh!

He shapes the trail
Carving with his blade
To say "hey" to his buddies
He just gives them a wave
Hello, hello
He loves the snow

In back the tiller
Treats the snow like its feast
While with wings on each side
He smooths the run like a beast
Woh -oh
Just watch him go

Hey, Hey, Hey!

With his special skills
He goes grooming all the hills
He's a Snowcat, oh!
Working through the night
Sculpting, shaping powder right
He's a Snowcat, oh, oh, oh, oh, oh!

He's well equipped
With gear and features galore
To make working more fun
For his operator
Woh -oh
They love the snow

Window defrosters
And so many controls
With his heated cab
Keeping out the cold
Oh, even tho-ough
It's ten belo-ow

Hey, Hey, Hey!

With his special skills
He goes grooming all the hills
He's a Snowcat, oh!
Working through the night

Sculpting, shaping powder right
He's a Snowcat, oh, oh, oh, oh, oh!
(Repeat)

FLATBED

Packs up with lumber and
    construction supplies
So his destination should come
    as no surprise
Yes, he's fully loaded up and tied
    down really tight
Making yet another run to the
    building site

His bed is flat, it's true
Makes loading easier
And unloading, too
Flatbed truck, why don't you
Show us all the many things you can do

For extra-big jobs, he takes a
    friend along
His buddy is the forklift and,
    well, she's pretty strong
Some Flatbeds even have a crane
    that's fully built right in
And without this feature, unloading
    won't begin

His bed is flat, it's true
Makes loading easier
And unloading, too

Flatbed truck, why don't you
Show us all the many things you can do

When loading's all done, he's got to be
    quite sure
His cargo's one hundred percent
    tightened and secure
He straps it all down and cinches it up
You bet you can be certain, he's one
    careful working truck

Oh, while you're certain to see
    Flatbeds in town
On freeways and on highways he'll
    also be around
No, he's not out there driving just
    to see the scenery
In fact, he's moving heavy, moving
    heavy machinery

His bed is flat, it's true
Makes loading easier
And unloading, too
Flatbed truck, why don't you
Show us all the many things you can do
(Repeat)

FOOD TRUCK

In some cities, in some towns
When these trucks all gather around
You can find any food you want
At these mobile restaurants

And some trucks like to keep
The same stops every week
While others like to mix it up
Today they might be here
Tomorrow they'll be there
To find 'em, you gotta look 'em up

Like a kitchen on wheels
Serving snacks, serving meals
For every kind of mood
A truck for every food

Get yourself a crunchy waffle
Or try out the falafel
He's a Food Truck, you know?
And he's always on the go

Equipped with ovens and big grills
Stovetops made of shiny steel
These trucks come all prepared
To cook up good food anywhere

It might occur to ask
Do they cook while driving fast?
The answer is a definite "no"
While they drive, the cook's on pause
'Cause they'd be breaking laws
If they kept cooking on the go

Like a kitchen on wheels
Serving snacks, serving meals
For every kind of mood
A truck for every food

Grab a gooey quesadilla
You'll love the sopapilla
He's a Food Truck, you know?
And he's always on the go
He's always on the go-o-o

It's true, these trucks have become
So, ooh, popular and some
Have even been featured on TV
But making great food isn't easy

So, you want to keep in mind
Some trucks have real long lines
And you just might have to wait a bit
So while waiting for your food
Be patient, don't be rude
Just remember it's your favorite
Umm, that looks delicious

Like a kitchen on wheels
Serving snacks, serving meals
For every kind of mood
A truck for every food

Score some spicy jambalaya
Or oh-so-fresh papaya
He's a Food Truck, you know?
And he's always on the go
He's always on the go-o-o

He's always on the go
He's always on the go-o-o

Like a kitchen on wheels
Serving snacks, serving meals
For every kind of mood
A truck for every food

Munch a bunch of crunchy nachos
A taste of tasty tacos
He's a Food Truck, you know?
And he's always on the go

OFF-ROAD RACING TRUCK

It's the Off-Road, Off-Road Racing Truck
Can you believe his amazing luck?
He's gotta keep tough
Gotta stay tuned up

Who's in the lead now?

Speeding through turns, he can't
    over-rotate
Hitting his jumps clean, not getting
    sideways, no
No time to be afraid, can't fear
    the contact
He only knows one mode:
Attack! Attack! Attack!

Who's in the lead now? Who's in the lead?

It's the Off-Road, Off-Road Racing Truck
Can you believe his amazing luck?
He's gotta keep tough
Gotta stay tuned up
And when things go wrong
He's gotta stay strong

Off-Road, Off-Road Racing Truck
And if he wins, he might make a buck
He's gotta keep tough
Gotta stay tuned up

Who's in the lead now?

She's rough and strong, she's as tough
    as can be
But if she wants first, then safety
    comes first, oh
When there's a crash on the track
A yellow flag gives warning
Wait for the green flag, then:
Go! Go! Go!

Who's in the lead now? Who's in the lead?

It's the Off-Road, Off-Road Racing Truck
Can you believe her amazing luck?
She's gotta keep tough
Gotta stay tuned up
And when things go wrong
She's gotta stay strong

Off-Road, Off-Road Racing Truck
And if she wins, she might make a buck

She's gotta keep tough
Gotta stay tuned up

Who's in the lead now? Who's in the lead?

They're strong! They're fast!
   They're stoked!
Racing is life, oh!
So, if you backfire:
Race on!
And if you lose a tire:
Race on!
Race on!

'Cause they're Off-Road, Off-Road
   Racing Trucks
Can you believe their amazing luck?
They gotta keep tough
Gotta stay tuned up
And when things go wrong
They gotta stay strong

Off-Road, Off-Road Racing Truck
And if they win, they might make a buck
They gotta keep tough
Gotta stay tuned up

Who's in the lead now?

WATER TRUCK

When there's dust on the job
When there's dirt at the site
It's a Water Truck's job
To keep dust minimized

Dirt is his nemesis
Dust is his foe
His job is to keep them both
Under control

Water cannon in front
Spray heads in back
Uses them all in
His water attack

'Cause when there's dust on the job
When there's dirt at the site
It's a Water Truck's job
To keep dust minimized

So, spray, spray, spray down the road
Oh, and spray, spray, spray down the site

This truck holds
Five thousand gallons when full
That's almost enough to
Fill a small swimming pool

Though that's a lot
Of capacity
While he works, he refills his
Tank frequently

'Cause when there's dust on the job
When there's dirt at the site
It's a Water Truck's job
To keep dust minimized

So, spray, spray, spray down the road
Oh, and spray, spray, spray down the site

Some call them Water Wagons
And some say Water Pulls
Regardless of the name
They've got lots and lots of tools

For doing their job well
There's just no doubt
Like this awesome water pump
That helps spray water out

When there's dust on the job
When there's dirt at the site
Oh, when there's dust on the job
When there's dirt at the site
It's a Water Truck's job
To keep dust minimized

So, spray, spray, spray down the road
Oh, and spray, spray, spray down the site

Yeah, we'll spray, spray, spray down
the road
Oh, and spray, spray, spray down the site

BUCKET WHEEL EXCAVATOR

Like a metal monster
That eats continuously
The Bucket Wheel Excavator
He digs so efficiently
With nearly a hundred
Percent availability
He's the perfect model
Of reliability

He's a nonstop operator
He's a digging dominator
He's a Bucket Wheel Excavator
Yeah, he's a Bucket Wheel Excavator

Some machines have booms, you know
Well, this Bucket Wheel has three
For cutting, for discharge
And a counterweight so heavy
With a crawler unit
He shows off his mobility
And with help from his friends he moves
His conveyor belt easily

Oh, he's a nonstop operator
He's a digging dominator
He's a Bucket Wheel Excavator
Yeah, he's a Bucket Wheel Excavator

He is one of the world's largest machines
Largest and strongest machines
He makes other very big trucks
Look like toys, like little playthings

'Cause he's a nonstop . . .

He's a nonstop operator
He's a digging dominator
He's a Bucket Wheel Excavator
Yeah, he's a Bucket Wheel Excavator

MILLING MACHINE

He's gonna grind, he's gonna crush up
  the street
He chews up the pavement like his
  favorite treat
You can call him Cold Planer or a
  Milling Machine
If you say Asphalt Grinder, we all know
  what you mean

When a road needs repairing
And simple patching won't do
He recycles the pavement
So it can be reused

A big rig carries him to the site
He unloads and prepares just right

He's very serious about his work

He's gonna grind, he's gonna crush up
  the street
He chews up the pavement like his
  favorite treat
You can call him Cold Planer or a
  Milling Machine
If you say Asphalt Grinder, we all know
  what you mean

He keeps his drum rotating
Grinding with carbide cutters
He cuts through the asphalt
Like a hot knife through butter

Water reduces dust and cools him down
His conveyor belt moves the road
  he's ground

And shoots it into a big dump truck

He's gonna grind, he's gonna crush up
  the street
He chews up the pavement like his
  favorite treat
You can call him Cold Planer or a
  Milling Machine
If you say Asphalt Grinder, we all know
  what you mean

ROCK CRAWLER

When you're rock crawlin'
Don't wanna be fallin'
'Cause when you're scalin'
It's so dangerous failin'

Rock Crawler
Rock Crawler

With all four wheels steerin'
There's no need to be fearin'
With tires so knobby
Rock grippin's more than a hobby

Rock Crawler
Rock Crawler
Rock Crawler
Rock Crawler

With awesome torque
She can carefully climb
Just about any
Rock she can find

Suspension gives her
The clearance she needs
Her differential transfers
Just the right speed

Body armor protects
The driver inside
A rollcage comes in handy
If she starts to slide

Rock Crawler
Rock Crawler

Those rocks, they are callin'
"Come do some rock crawlin'"
Those stones keep insisting
Oh, there's no use in resisting

Rock Crawler
Rock Crawler
Rock Crawler
Rock Crawler

BACKHOE

He's like a loader, and a digger and a
  grader, too
There aren't many jobs that this truck
  can't do
To switch from one to the other is
  easy, so
Push the button and to work you go

And for all his capabilities
They call him Mr. Versatility, yeah!

If you've got a tough job that you need
  to do
Where an excavator 'n' loader wouldn't
  have room
Just let him know, and he'll be there
He can do so much, some say it isn't fair

'Cause for all his capabilities
They call him Mr. Versatility, yeah!

His two stabilizers keep him steady, so
To scoop a load, he's always ready to go
You can move him around using
  his controls
Spend all day just digging holes

And for all his capabilities
They call him Mr. Versatility, yeah!

Now, don't forget, he can also load
Filling this dump truck, working on
  the road
If you see him at work, you might want
  to say:
"Mom and Dad, I saw a Backhoe today!"

And for all his capabilities
They call him Mr. Versatility, yeah!

Look, here, this truck is his little bro'
He's a miniature version of this Backhoe
He can do anything that his brother
  can do
'Cause he's smaller, he can work in
  tighter places, too

And for all his capabilities
They call him Mini Versatility, yeah!

And for all his capabilities
They call him Mr. Versatility
Yeah!

ICE RESURFACING MACHINE

Watch the people out there on the ice
They glide as they skate round and round
But the more that they skate and they
 skate and they skate
Then the ice becomes rough on
 the ground

That's when this truck comes around for
 his turn
His job is to smoo-ooth out the ice
He goes up and around, then around
 once again
Till the rink is all perfect and nice

Oh, he's the Ice Resurfacing Machine
He smooths out all the ice
Makes it skate twice as nice
Makes the rink so perfect and clean
An ingenious device to resurface the ice

Oh, he shaves off the ice with a blade
A blade with an edge razor thin
Then the augers, like big screws, they
 turn and they turn
And they carry the ice to a bin

All while the wash water shoots from
 the jets
To clean off the snow and debris
This is vacuumed and cleaned, and then
 cleaned once again
With the help of a big giant squeegee

He's the Ice Resurfacing Machine
He smooths out all the ice
Makes it skate twice as nice
Makes the rink so perfect and clean
An ingenious device to resurface the ice

Recirculated water sprays out
Oh, so hot!
Then smoothed with a towel

So, the hot water melts
All the ice down below
Makes it strong, makes it smooth
More like ice than like snow . . .

How many snow cones
Do you think you could make
With the ice he collects in his tank?

This one right here shaves enough ice in one resurfacing to make more than 3600 snow cones!
That's a lot of snow cones!

He's the Ice Resurfacing Machine
He smooths out all the ice
Makes it skate twice as nice
Makes the rink so perfect and clean
An ingenious device to resurface the ice

Happy skating, everyone!

BEACH CLEANER

When you're cleaning the beach
He's always happy to help
Moving litter and junk
And a whole lot of kelp

He cleans the beach
He cleans the beach, oh yeah
He works as fast as he can
So you can play in the sand
He cleans the beach

He goes out in the morning
The beach almost empty
Works the controls to get
The digger depth set

He may look pretty slow
But he's working hard, you know
The conveyor scoops sand
So it can be fully screened
The debris sifted out
By this awesome machine

He cleans the beach
He cleans the beach, oh yeah
He works as fast as he can
So you can play in the sand
He cleans the beach

You might be surprised
By what he can find
As he steadily moves up
And down the shoreline

Oh, there's wrappers and bags
And yeah, all kinds of trash
But he also gets jewelry
Or the phone you can't find
He may dig up some cash
Or someone's ring left behind

He cleans the beach
He cleans the beach, oh yeah
He works as fast as he can
So you can play in the sand
He cleans the beach

He has just three wheels
So his turns are real tight
And with those three wheels
He cleans fire pits right

When his hopper's all full
He can lift it up high
And then he dumps all that junk
In a container nearby
Then he goes cleaning
He's back at it again

He's always cleaning
Makes the beach spic and span

'Cause when you're cleaning the beach
He's always happy to help
Moving litter and junk
And a whole lot of kelp

He cleans the beach
He cleans the beach, oh yeah
He works as fast as he can

So you can play in the sand
He cleans the beach
He cleans, he cleans the beach
He cleans, he cleans the beach
He cleans, he cleans the beach

He works as fast as he can
So you can play in the sand
He cleans the beach

He cleans, he cleans the beach

ICE CREAM TRUCK

If you're like me then
When you hear him play that tune
You know exactly what it means
On a hot afternoon

You keep a look out
Don't wanna miss out
I hope you saved some room
You hear his song
And hurry quickly, join the queue
You make your choice and then you
Take your money, pay him too

And then you chill out
Try not to spill out
I hope you saved some room
I hope you saved some room for

Ice cream
Cool me down, cool me down with
Ice cream
Turn my frown upside down with
Ice cream
All around through the town
The Ice Cream Truck goes round
   and round

You're at the park and suddenly you
Hear your favorite sound
It's about the only thing
That'll make you leave the playground
He's in the neighborhood
His treats are frozen good
I hope he'll come around

He's fully stocked with
Treats and goodies oh so cold
He loads 'em up, and settles in
And heads out on the road

Will it be Sunday?
Or maybe Monday?
I hope he'll come around
I hope he'll come around with

Ice cream
Cool me down, cool me down with
Ice cream
Turn my frown upside down with
Ice cream
All around through the town
The Ice Cream Truck goes round and . . .

Cools the freezer overnight
Gotta get the temperature just right
To keep 'em frozen 'ight

The only problem might just be
You have to choose
Do you take the cone, the ice
   cream sandwich?
Can you even lose?
Oh, what an obstacle
Do you pick the popsicle?

How are you gonna choose?
How are you gonna choose your

Ice cream
Cool me down, cool me down with
Ice cream
Turn my frown upside down with
Ice cream
All around through the town
The Ice Cream Truck goes round
   and round

SCRAPER

There's a truck who works real hard
Building roads for people's cars
So you'll have a place to drive around on
He sure loves to dig, dig, dig
Building homes where you can live
He's the truck you know that you can
    count on

If you've got a lot of dirt you need to move
    around
You can count on Scraper
Watch him cruising really fast to scrape up
    other ground
'Cause you can count on Scraper

He's building a new community
These roads will soon be running streams
The water from the streams will make a
    lake here
Then homes will sprout up from
    the ground
Homes wherever you look around
Many kids like you will call it home here

Oh, if you've got a lot of dirt you need to
    move around
You can count on Scraper

Watch him as he digs and watch him as he
    shapes the ground
Yeah, you can count on Scraper

Now here's something you might
    not know
Where dirt is held is called the bowl
And where it opens up is called
    the apron
It opens up to take a load
And fills with dirt that leaves a hole
The ejector shoves it out so he can
    start again

So, if you've got a lot of dirt you need to
    move around
You can count on Scraper
Watch him cruising really fast to scrape up
    other ground
'Cause you can count on Scraper
(Repeat)

After a short break for lunch
They rumble out and I've a hunch
They'll be working all day long till
    night fall
If you see him while you're out
Maybe you could call and shout
"Hey, there goes a Scraper! I can
    count on him."

'Cause, if you've got a lot of dirt you need to move around
You can count on Scraper
Watch him cruising really fast to scrape up other ground
'Cause you can count on Scraper

Oh, if you've got a lot of dirt you need to move around
You can count on Scraper
Watch him as he digs and watch him as he shapes the ground
Yeah, you can count on Scraper

GRADER

Have you ever seen a truck like this?
Working the job, they're kinda hard
    to miss
If you know his name, well you can shout it
    out now
And if you said "Grader," well all I can say
    is "Wow!"

Some people call them Graders
Some people call them Blades
They're very good at getting the road
Readied up to pave

And when it's very cold outside
And there is lots of snow
You may see one cruising by
Using its blade to clear the road

The main part of the Grader is
This straight blade you see here
One side in front of the other as
The driver sits and steers

The front is called the toe
And the back is called the heel
The blade's job is to level out
The dirt behind the forward wheels

Have you ever seen a truck like this?
Working the job, they're kinda hard
    to miss
If you know his name, well you can shout it
    out now
And if you said "Grader," well all I can say
    is "Wow!"

Here's a special feature that
Many trucks don't have
If you watch real close
Then you're sure to understand

The front wheel goes right up
And over this great mound
While the blade stays where it is
Nice and level with the ground

Another of this truck's
Very unique abilities
Is to do a special trick
It's called a "wheel lean"

By leaning his wheels just a bit
Or even quite a lot
The Grader operator here
Can control how his blade cuts

So, have you ever seen a truck like this?
Working the job, they're kinda hard
to miss

If you know his name, you can whisper
it now
If you said "Grader," well all I can say is
"Good Job!"

MAIL TRUCK

Go on and send me a letter
'Cause nobody does it better
Than a Mail Truck
Than a Mail Truck
Go on and ship me a package
And they'll carry it in back of
This-a Mail Truck
This-a Mail Truck

They come by your house
Most days of the week
Move deliberately
Along each side of the street
They won't stop
These trucks just won't stop
Making deliveries
They keep moving along
Till their route is complete
'Cause these trucks just won't stop
They won't stop, no

The Mail Truck's so reliable
Their look so recognizable
They're determined and methodical
They get the job done, it's undeniable

Go on and send me a letter
'Cause nobody does it better
Than a Mail Truck

Than a Mail Truck
Go on and ship me a package
And they'll carry it in back of
This-a Mail Truck
This-a Mail Truck

The carrier drives
On the right side, you see
To deliver the mail without
Leaving their seat
They won't stop
No, they just won't stop
Maneuvers easily
The truck's turning radius
Shows their mobility
'Cause these trucks just won't stop
They won't stop, no

They're designed for longevity
Long Life Vehicle, LLV
Most are twenty years old at least
Working day after day, continuously

More than one hundred thousand
   of these
Out running in the mail carrier fleet
Carrying millions of items each day
Delivering billions of packages
Wouldn't you say?

The Mail Truck's so reliable
Their look so recognizable
They're determined and methodical
They get the job done, it's undeniable

Go on and send me a letter
'Cause nobody does it better

Than a Mail Truck
Than a Mail Truck
Go on and ship me a package
And they'll carry it in back of
This-a Mail Truck
This-a Mail Truck
(Repeat)

DELIMBER

These are the ABC and Ds
Of the truck whose job it is
To clean all of the cut-down trees
Of their limbs and of their branches

ABCDEFG
HIJKLMNOP
QRSTUVWXYZ

Scraping **A**ll the **B**ranches off
Cutting the trees with a muffled roar
Sucking logs into his mouth
Like a mechanical **D**inosaur

Powered by a big **E**ngine
He picks up all the trees the
Feller Buncher set down on the **G**round
And prepares them to be **H**auled
Hauled into the town

Oh, A is for All the wood he chews
And B is for the Branches he removes
Now C is for the Cuts that he delivers
And D, the letter D is for Delimber

To prevent an **I**njury
It's best to stay far back from him
Logs can **J**ump up or **K**ick back
When he is removing **L**imbs

To see how wide these big trees are
And cut them just the perfect size
Some Delimbers **M**easure them
It's a **N**oisy **O**peration
Working in the **P**ines

Oh, A is for All the wood he chews
And B is for the Branches he removes
Now C is for the Cuts that he delivers
And D, the letter D is for Delimber

Now where were we? At letter Q?
Well let's go then!

They can work oh so **Q**uickly
Rarely taking vacations
Using chain **S**aws just like **T**eeth
In these forest locations

Delimbers are so very **U**seful
And so **V**aluable too
The logs they cut become our **W**ood
And oh so many kinds of paper
For you and me to use

Oh, A is for All the wood he chews
And B is for the Branches he removes
Now C is for the Cuts that he delivers
And D, the letter D is for Delimber

Delimbers are so e**X**cellent
Working almost all **Y**ear round
In any logging or timber **Z**one
If you'll do no more than look
They're certain to be found

Oh, A is for All the wood he chews
And B is for the Branches he removes
Now C is for the Cuts that he delivers
Oh, and D, the letter D
Yes, D the letter D
Oh, D the letter D Is for Delimber

I LOVE TRUCKS

Guess what makes me so happy?
I love trucks and big machines
Guess what makes me so happy?
I love trucks and big machines

'Cause they're so big
And incredibly strong
'Cause they never get tired
And work all day long

'Cause they have cool parts
Like their hoppers and booms
'Cause some move real slow
And some seriously zoom

Can't help put a smile on my face
Watch them moving and working all day

Guess what makes me so happy?
I love trucks and big machines
Guess what makes me so happy?
I love trucks and big machines

'Cause they scrape and dig
And they rattle the ground
'Cause they grumble and roar
And make all kinds of sounds

'Cause they can reach low
Or lift high in the sky
'Cause they clean up a mess
In a single drive-by

'Cause they're not afraid
To go from coast to coast
'Cause pulling and hauling
Is what they like the most

Can't help put a smile on my face
Watch them moving and working all day

'Cause they dig and they smash
And they clean and they haul

'Cause they build and tear down
'Cause they're tough and they're tall
They dig and they smash
And they clean and they haul

They build and tear down
And they're tough and they're tall

Guess what makes me so happy?
I love trucks and big machines
Guess what makes me so happy?
I love trucks and big machines
Guess what makes me so happy?
I love trucks and big machines

GLOSSARY OF TRUCK TERMS

Articulated: a truck or part of a truck that has two or more sections connected by a flexible joint. The long, articulated arms of a concrete boom pump have multiple sections connected by joints.

Auger: a tool with a spiral shaft used for boring holes or moving loose material. Ice resurfacers use an internal auger to move ice from the blade to the bin.

Boom: a long beam or arm that supports a load, like the arm that an excavator uses to dig with his bucket.

Capacity: the largest amount that something can hold, such as a cement mixer drum or a water truck tank.

Compact: to exert force on something to make it smaller and denser. Garbage trucks compact the trash in their hoppers.

Conveyor: a mechanical handling system that moves materials from one location to another. Road zippers use a conveyor to move the heavy concrete sections to create a barrier wall for traffic.

Concrete: a material that is composed of cement, water, and an aggregate (like broken rock or gravel) that hardens over time.

Counterweight: a weight that applies force on one side of a truck to provide stability. Forklifts have a counterweight in back to prevent them from tipping over when lifting heavy loads.

Debris: pieces of litter, waste, or wreckage that are scattered around, such as at a work site or alongside a road. Street sweepers clean up debris to keep the streets clean.

Hopper: a container for bulk materials that typically narrows as it goes down. Pavers load hot asphalt into a hopper on one side to pave a street.

Hydraulic: operated or powered by pressurized liquid. Dump truck beds are lifted and lowered by hydraulics.

Pallet: a flat, wooden structure that supports goods to make moving or storage easier. The blades of a forklift fit neatly into pallets to lift and carry them from one place to another.

Telescoping: an object made of tube-like parts that can slide into each other to make that object shorter or longer. Truck cranes use their telescoping booms to reach high into the sky.

Ton: a unit of weight equal to 2,000 pounds. Large excavators can dig up many tons of dirt in one scoop of their bucket.

Tractor: a vehicle designed to pull or haul trailers or other machinery. Semi-trucks are made up of two main parts: a tractor and a trailer. This is why they are also called tractor trailers.

Truck: a large, heavy vehicle used for transporting materials, goods, or people.

Viscous: the thick consistency between a liquid and a solid. Cement trucks rotate their drums while they drive to help keep the concrete inside viscous and to prevent it from hardening too early.

Winch: a lifting or hauling device made up of a cable, chain, or rope that winds around a rotating drum. Tow trucks use winches to help load up cars so they can be towed.

Yard of concrete: an amount of ready-mix concrete equal to one cubic yard, or 3x3x3 feet. Some concrete boom pumps can pump more than a hundred yards of concrete per hour.

JIM and **ROB GARDNER** write and produce the *Truck Tunes* music videos, which feature real work machines in action. The music videos are fun, educational, and appeal to kids of all ages. Since the release of the first *Truck Tunes*, Jim and Rob have produced more than sixty truck songs and the videos have millions of views on the TwentyTrucks channel on YouTube.

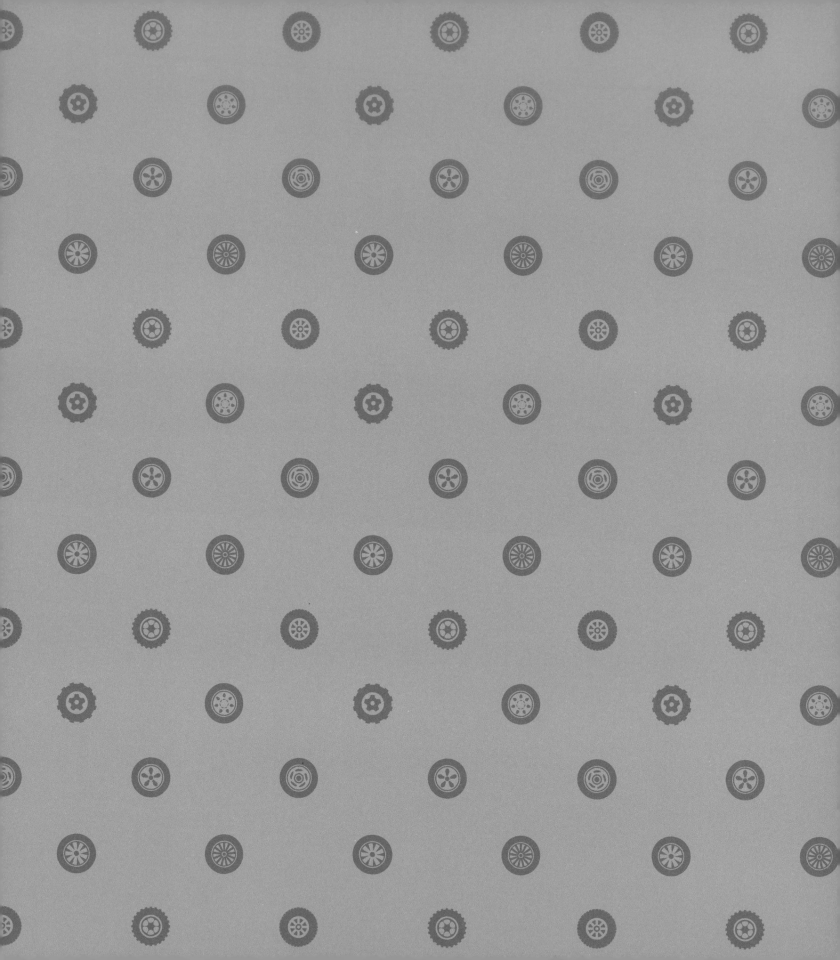